DANCE

Lucy Smith

Edited by Helen Davies and Pam Beasant

Designed by Nerissa Davies

Contents

Dance Consultants: Jan Murray, Bronwyn Williams, Warren Hayes, Terry Monahan, Sue Davies, Patrick Duncan, Colin Holsgrove and Jeannette Mac Donald

Illustrated by Kathy James, Chris Lyon, Mick Posen, Sue Stitt, Cathy Wood, Nerissa Davies and Gordon Lawson

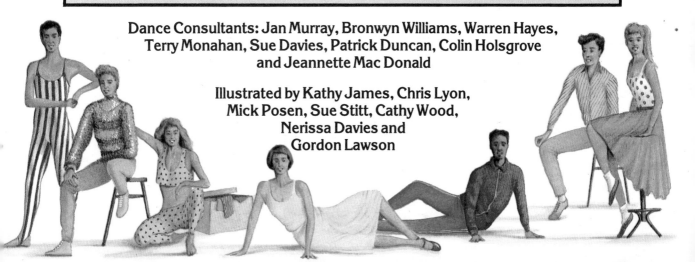

About dance

All over the world people have always danced. Dancing is a way of expressing moods and feelings by making shapes with your body and moving in a rhythmical way. In many countries, dance is an important part of the culture and special occasions are often accompanied by dancing.

In this book you can find out about lots of different kinds of dance, in particular those shown below.

Contemporary dance

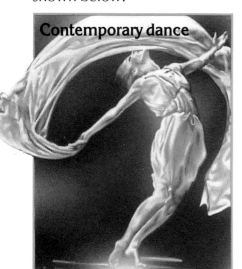

Contemporary dance began at the start of this century when Isadora Duncan broke away from ballet and invented a very individual style of dancing. Another American dancer, Martha Graham, developed a contemporary dance technique which is now taught in many classes.

Jazz dance

Jazz dance first developed with jazz music in the 1920s. In the 1950s, as popular music changed, so did jazz dance. Today there are many different styles of jazz, danced to various kinds of music. They all feature energetic and rhythmical movement. To do jazz you need to be fit and supple.

Tap dance

The movements of tap are concentrated in your feet. Wearing shoes with metal toe-caps, you tap out the rhythm of the music you are dancing to. To tap dance you do not have to be as fit as you do for some other kinds of dance, but you need to move in a flowing, graceful way.

Popular dances

Popular dances are done with other people and not necessarily to entertain an audience. Disco dancing, body popping, breakdancing and rock 'n' roll are all popular dances. You can find out more about them and learn some of their basic steps later in the book.

Why dance?

There are lots of good reasons to dance. It gives you a healthier body, it makes you feel happy and confident and it can be very exciting to do. It is also great fun to dance with friends. You can dance to almost any music you like, as long as it has a good rhythm.

Learning to dance

There are classes in almost every kind of dance, and you can learn popular styles such as disco by watching other people. You do not have to be very fit to start dancing, nor do you need an expensive new wardrobe of clothes. All you need are clothes which let you move freely.

Learning to dance for fun does not take long, but if you want to be very good or professional you will need to devote a lot of time to it.

TIME	STYLE	LEVEL	HRS
9.30	JAZZ	BEGINNER	1
10.00	AMERICAN TAP	INTERMEDIATE	2
12.30	BALLET	INTERMEDIATE	2½
1.00	ROCK JAZZ	BEGINNER	1
2.00	CEROC	BEGINNER	1
3.00	FLAMENCO DANCING	ADVANCED	1½
4.00	CONTEMPORARY	INTERMEDIATE/ADVANCED	1½
5.00	BELLY DANCING	BEGINNER	1

TIMETABLE MONDAY

About this book

In this book you can find out how the different types of dance began and developed, and the famous dancers associated with them. You can learn about creating dances and about how music and dance go together. There are also some simple moves and steps for you to try yourself.

Classes

The book explains what happens at a dance class and how to prepare your body for dance. There are hints on what to wear too.

Companies

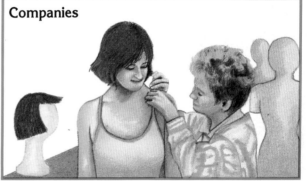

You can find out about dance companies and the different jobs people do, such as designing and making dancers' costumes.

Staging

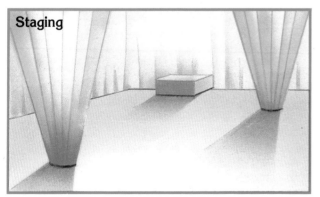

You can also see how a dance is prepared for the stage, or "staged", from designing the set to creating lighting effects.

Sport

Ice-skating and gymnastics are sports which use dance movements. You can find out about this in the last part of the book.

Preparing to dance

Dancing makes great demands on your body. Before you start any dance session, you should do some warm-up exercises. These are gentle exercises which help to loosen and stretch your muscles and prepare them for more vigorous work. If you do not warm up your body, you may damage a muscle while you are dancing. There are some warm-up exercises to try on pages 6-7.

It is also important to cool down gradually after dancing. This is to allow your muscles to recover and your pulse rate to return to normal.

What to wear

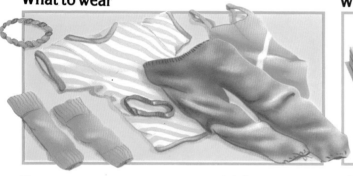

To warm up, you can wear any clothes that are comfortable and allow you to move freely. Clothes made from natural fibres are good because they are warmer and absorb sweat. It is best to warm up either in bare feet or soft dance slippers.

If you have long hair, tie it back. Remove any jewellery that is likely to get caught or that might scratch you.

Where and when to dance

Linoleum → A "sprung" floor is made of wooden boards which give when you jump on them.

Wooden boards resting on joists.

Ideally you should go to a class at a dance studio with a sprung wooden floor, varnished or covered with linoleum to prevent splinters. Never dance on very hard floors, such as concrete, as this jars your joints.

At home, exercise on a carpeted or smooth, clean floor. Try to wait two hours after a meal before dancing, or you may get stomach cramps.

Why muscles need warming up

The muscles used for moving are made up of long, thin strands of tissue known as muscle fibres. These fibres cannot replace themselves if they are damaged. Warm-up exercises stretch the muscle fibres slightly and prepare them for harder work.

Muscle → ← Bundle of muscle fibres

Breathing

When you exercise you need to breathe using both the lower and the upper parts of your lungs. To check you are doing this place one hand on your stomach and the other on your chest. As you inhale, you should feel your stomach move first, then your chest.

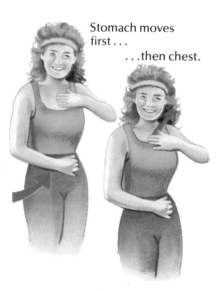

Stomach moves first . . .
. . . then chest.

Checking your pulse

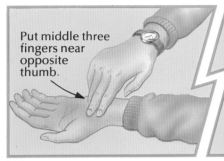

Put middle three fingers near opposite thumb.

HOW TO CALCULATE YOUR MAXIMUM PULSE RATE:

220 — (YOUR AGE) = YOUR APPROXIMATE MAXIMUM PULSE RATE

E.G. IF YOU ARE AGED 10:
220 — 10 = 210

TO CALCULATE 3/5 OF YOUR MAXIMUM PULSE RATE:

E.G. IF YOUR MAXIMUM PULSE RATE IS 210:

$$\frac{3}{5} \times 210 = \frac{3 \times 210}{5}$$
$$= \frac{630}{5} = 126$$

Your pulse shows the rate at which the blood is pumped round your body. To take your pulse you need a watch which shows seconds. Put the middle three fingers of one hand on the wrist of the other hand. Count how many times your pulse beats in fifteen seconds and multiply this by four.

To find out how well you are exercising you need to compare your pulse rate with your "maximum pulse rate". This is the highest number of times your heart could beat in a minute.

When you exercise, you will get the most benefit if your pulse rate rises to about 3/5 or 60% of its

maximum rate. Never make your pulse rise to more than 4/5 or 80% of the maximum level, as this puts too much strain on your heart.

Take your pulse just before and just after each exercise session and keep a record of how much the rate has increased.

Posture

Your posture is the way you hold yourself, whether standing, sitting or lying down. Good posture is very important for dance, as it helps you move and look better.

For good posture, your shoulders should be relaxed and level, your head up and your spine straight. Try the exercise on the right to improve your posture.

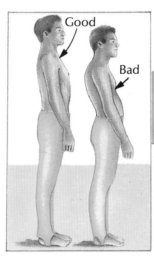

Good

Bad

Posture exercise

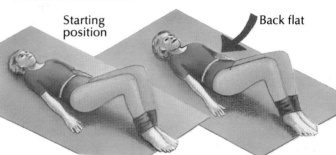

Starting position

Back flat

Lie on a carpet with your knees bent and pressed together. Place your hands by your thighs and keep your feet parallel and flat on the floor.

Try to make the whole of your back touch the floor. Relax your shoulders. Don't bend your neck - keep it "long" (stretched out straight).

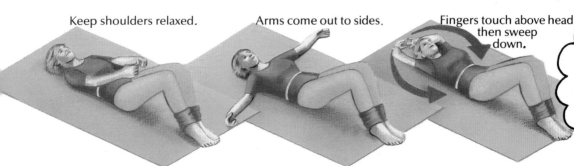

Keep shoulders relaxed.

Arms come out to sides.

Fingers touch above head then sweep down.

To improve your posture, do this exercise regularly, repeating it four times.

Breathe in deeply. At the same time, form your arms into an oval in front of you, with your fingers touching below your waist. Keep the rest of your body still.

Breathe out slowly, pushing your stomach towards the floor and sweeping each arm out sideways in a wide arc. Try to keep your back flat.

Still breathing out, continue moving your arms up to form an oval above your head. Then sweep them down in an arc to the starting position.

5

Warm-up exercises

Here are some warm-up exercises to try. Repeat each of them three or four times.

Take care not to overdo it though. If any muscles feel painful afterwards, soaking in a warm bath should ease them. If the muscles are very painful for several days, see your doctor.

Checklist for warming up

1 Wear loose, comfortable clothes.

2 Exercise in a warm place where there is plenty of space.

3 Exercise on a carpeted or sprung wood floor.

4 Before you start check your posture and practise breathing properly (see pages 4-5).

Remember, while doing these exercises, try to keep your stomach pulled in, your back straight and your bottom tucked in.
Don't worry if you can't manage all this at first. Keep trying, and have fun.

The centre of movement

Your centre of movement is the dance term for the mid-point of your body where all dance moves begin.

Knowing where your centre of movement is helps you keep your balance when you are dancing. If you pull in your stomach and imagine that it is touching your spine, the point where it touches is your centre.

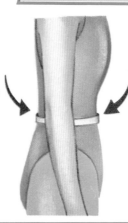

Warming up your feet

Your feet bear all your weight, so they need to be supple, especially when you are dancing. To warm them up, find a smooth pole or broom handle. Sit up straight on a hard chair. Place the pole on the floor in front of you and put one foot on it. Roll the foot forwards and backwards, keeping it on the pole. Then do the same with the other foot.

Head roll

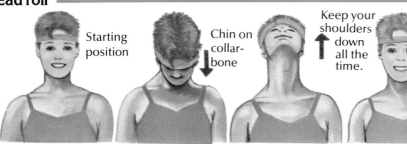

Starting position

Chin on collar-bone

Keep your shoulders down all the time.

Stand with feet slightly apart, back straight and shoulders down. Look straight ahead.

Tilt your head forwards. Then tilt it back slowly, opening your mouth. Then close your mouth.

Centre your head again, then tilt it forwards. Then return to centre again smoothly.

Turn your head to the right and return to centre. Then turn it to the left and return to centre.

Shoulder shrugs

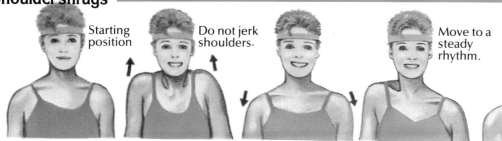

Starting position

Do not jerk shoulders.

Move to a steady rhythm.

Stand in the starting position (see head roll), arms hanging loosely by your sides.

Lift both shoulders towards your ears, then push them down. Repeat four times.

Now raise your shoulders alternately so that when one is up the other is down, like a seesaw.

Return to the starting position after each movement. Repeat four times.

Arm swings

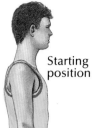 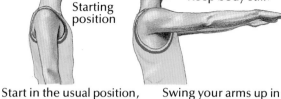 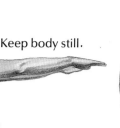 

Start in the usual position, but with your feet slightly further apart for balance.

Swing your arms up in front of you to shoulder height. Then return them to your sides.

Next, swing them out sideways to shoulder height. Then return them to your sides.

Now revolve your arms in two big backward circles. Try to keep the rest of your body still.

Waist bend

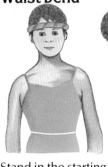 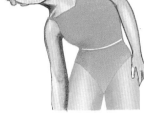 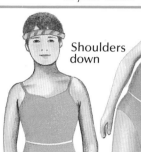 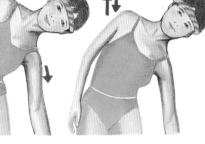

Stand in the starting position, with feet quite wide apart, arms relaxed.

Bend sideways to the right, sliding your right arm down your right leg.*

Return to centre. Bend to the left, with your left arm sliding down your left leg.

Holding the bent position, bounce up and down from the waist four times.

Waist twist

 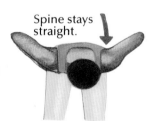 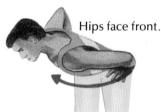 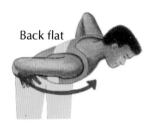

Stand in the starting position, but with your hands on your hips. Bend forwards from the waist.

Keep your upper body parallel with the floor and your back flat. Don't bend your neck.

Slowly revolve your upper body, or torso, to the right from the waist. Keep your hips still.

Revolve your torso to the left in the same way. Repeat to each side four times.

Leg stretches

  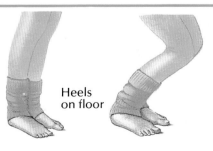 

Stand in the starting position but with your hands on your hips and your feet together.

Rise up on the balls of your feet. Then bring your heels back down so you return to the start.

Immediately bend your knees as far as you can, while keeping your heels flat on the floor.

You should feel your calf muscles stretch as your knees bend. Now straighten up again.

*When you repeat this exercise, start by bending to the left.

Learning to dance

If you want to learn contemporary, jazz or tap dance, you will need to take classes. To make good progress you must attend regularly. One class a week is enough for a beginner, but if you want to be a really good dancer you will have to build up to three classes a week or more. You can find out more about taking dance classes on these two pages.

Most people pick up popular dances such as rock 'n' roll or breakdancing at discos and parties. It is possible to take classes in these styles, but you may have to hunt around to find them.

Choosing a dance class

Before paying for a course of classes, ask if you can watch one first. This will help you decide whether you like this type of dance, and whether you enjoy the teacher's approach. If possible, take a friend who has some dancing experience when you first go to watch a class.

Some dance studios let you take one or two trial classes before registering for a full course.

Check that the teacher has proper qualifications. He or she should be trained as a professional dance teacher, or should have danced with a good professional dance company.

Training your body

Learning to dance well is hard work. There may be times when your muscles hurt and you feel that you are not getting anywhere. But don't be discouraged. Even professional dancers have to face up to disappointments sometimes.

Don't overdo your training, especially at first. You are more likely to lose heart if you tire yourself out. When you practise at home, be careful: it is best just to do simple warm-up exercises (see pages 6-7), or moves which you have learnt in class.

Follow the tips on pages 4-5 about looking after your muscles. Remember, although dancing is a discipline, it should also be fun.

At a dance class

Each dance teacher has his or her own teaching style, but most dance classes are divided into stages. In some kinds of dance, for example contemporary, the classes follow quite a strict pattern. For other styles classes are less formal.

It is a good idea to get to the class early so you can do your own warm-up exercises before it starts.

During the class your teacher will probably move round the studio to see how each student is getting on. Don't be afraid to ask the teacher to show you how to do a movement again if you are not sure about it.

A contemporary class

One of the most common contemporary dance techniques is Graham technique (see pages 12-13), named after Martha Graham.

A Graham class is divided into three stages. The class starts with "floorwork". This involves doing simple exercises either sitting or lying on the floor. These help to increase the suppleness of your spine and limbs.

The second stage of a Graham class is called centrework. You do exercises standing up, but staying in one place. These help you develop better balance and a sense of your centre of movement.

The third stage of a Graham class involves moving in space. This means doing travelling steps, and sequences which help your co-ordination.

A jazz class

In a jazz class you start with warm-up exercises. You then do exercises to improve your sense of rhythm, which is very important for jazz dance. Part of the class also involves learning isolations. An isolation is the movement of one part of your body separately from the rest of it. Isolations are a vital part of jazz dance.

In the last part of the class you usually do a sequence of movements which has been worked out, or choreographed, by the teacher. The sequence is built up gradually, starting off with simple steps. As your dancing improves, the sequence gets more complicated and different movements are added.

A tap class

The first part of a tap class concentrates on warming up your feet by bouncing up and down and jumping.

You then do basic steps, such as forward and backward taps, to fairly slow rhythms. This allows you to practise doing the steps using the correct part of the foot.

Then you work to a faster rhythm and combine the basic moves to make patterns of fast steps called time steps. You learn various routines, which you repeat and add to at each class. You may also spend part of the class learning to dance in time to music and with a partner.

A rock 'n' roll class

In the first class you learn how to hold your partner and how to move your feet in time to the music.

You warm up and get used to working with a partner by doing exercises like holding both hands and bouncing on the spot together. This helps the two of you to co-ordinate your movements, ready for doing more difficult routines.

Then you start learning rock 'n' roll moves, such as twirls and spins. Rock 'n' roll dancing is made up of sequences of these moves fitted into the rhythm of the steps you are doing with your feet. As you progress the moves become more complex and energetic.

In each class you practise the basic moves and learn some new ones.

Contemporary dance

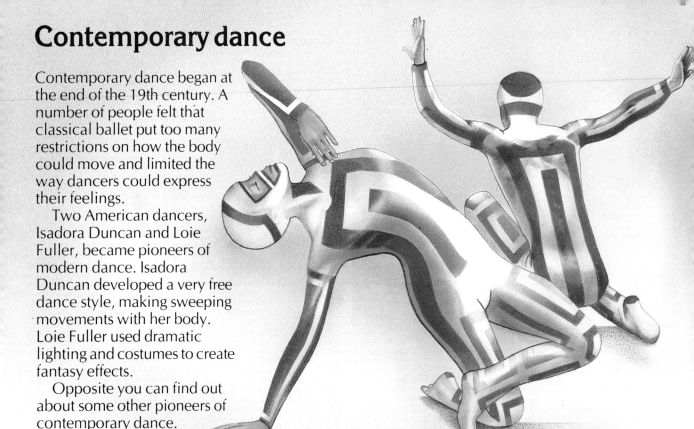

Contemporary dance began at the end of the 19th century. A number of people felt that classical ballet put too many restrictions on how the body could move and limited the way dancers could express their feelings.

Two American dancers, Isadora Duncan and Loie Fuller, became pioneers of modern dance. Isadora Duncan developed a very free dance style, making sweeping movements with her body. Loie Fuller used dramatic lighting and costumes to create fantasy effects.

Opposite you can find out about some other pioneers of contemporary dance.

The aims of contemporary dance

Contemporary dance is concerned with expressing your own feelings, so it is a very flexible kind of dance. Because feelings and thoughts vary from person to person, contemporary dancers continually explore and discover new ways of moving. They do not have to keep to a fixed technique.

Men and women have equal importance on the contemporary dance stage. They do not have to fit into traditional roles as they usually do in classical ballet. Below you can see some differences between classical ballet and contemporary dance.

	Ballet		Contemporary dance
1	The shapes and patterns the dancers make nearly always look graceful and beautiful.	1	Dance can show the ugly as well as the beautiful things that exist in life.
2	The body must be a particular size and shape, and is trained from a young age to achieve this.	2	The body can be any weight and height provided it is strong and supple.
3	Dancers look light and leap through the air as if they are defying gravity.	3	Many movements are based on the floor. Dancers use the pull of gravity to tilt and fall.
4	The basic steps are strictly defined. Every dancer learns these movements.	4	There are many different styles of dancing which require various sorts of training.
5	Dances usually follow a story line and include different characters.	5	Dances are often about ideas or moods, instead of telling a definite story.
6	Dancers wear special clothes, such as tutus, which show their movements clearly. Women wear special shoes for dancing on *pointes* (tiptoe).	6	Dancers wear all sorts of different clothes. They may wear very casual or very elaborate costumes. They often dance barefoot.

The Denishawn School

In 1914 two American dancers called Ruth St. Denis and Ted Shawn founded a dance-school called the Denishawn School. Their dancing was modern and very theatrical. The school taught dance styles from all over the world, for instance Japanese dance. It encouraged dancers to invent new techniques.

Many students from Denishawn went on to become pioneers of contemporary dance.

Martha Graham

Martha Graham was a student at the Denishawn School. She developed her own contemporary dance technique and in 1927 founded the Martha Graham school in New York.

She also became famous for her dramatic dance performances (see page 36). Her style contrasted very closed-in positions with free and open ones. Many contemporary dance schools now teach a technique based on hers.

Rudolf von Laban

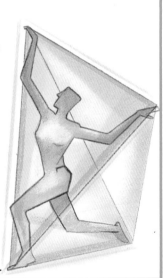

Rudolf von Laban's ideas influenced modern dance styles in the 1920s. Laban was a teacher and creator of dances working in Germany. He analyzed movement in a scientific way to show how it could express things more clearly.

His geometric sketches showed how different gestures like reaching out or crouching down could change the way the body fitted into a space.

Merce Cunningham

Merce Cunningham is an American dancer whose work has had a big impact on contemporary dance. After working with Martha Graham, he founded his own dance group in 1953. It is now one of the most famous contemporary dance companies in the world.

Cunningham's style combines elegance with natural movements to create a flowing and relaxed effect.

Post-modern dance

Post-modern dance first emerged in New York in the 1960s. The term refers to the various experimental forms of contemporary dance which have developed since then.

Some post-modern ideas about dance include the use of improvisation (when dancers make up the movements on the spot), speech, video and film in dances. Post-modern dances have been performed in unusual places, such as art galleries.

New styles of dance are always being developed as contemporary dancers experiment with different ways of moving.

11

Graham-based exercises

These pages show some contemporary dance exercises for you to try. They are based on Martha Graham's technique and are divided into floorwork, centrework, and moving in space (see page 9).

As you do each movement, try to concentrate on how it feels. Picture to yourself what you are trying to do, as shown on the right. Repeat each exercise several times using both sides of your body.

To help you keep your back and neck straight, imagine you are being pulled up by a string tied to the top of your head.

Floorwork

Floorwork exercises are done sitting, kneeling or lying down. They help you control your body better and make your spine supple. Since you stay in one place and move slowly, floorwork exercises help you to concentrate on your body and how each movement feels.

Try to use the floor as a working surface: don't just lean on it, but push down against it to give more strength to your movements.

Sitting spine stretch

Relax head and neck.

You may not be able to bend this far at first.

Sit with your knees bent and the soles of your feet pressed together. Rest your hands on your ankles and keep your back straight.

Bend forwards slowly as far as you can, breathing out. Keep your bottom on the floor and your legs still. Then straighten up slowly.

Parallel leg flexes

Keep left leg straight.

Keep back straight.

Sit with your legs and arms parallel and straight out in front. Point your feet.

Bend your right knee, flexing, or bending, the right foot towards you. Return to the start.

Do the same exercise but flex the left foot and point the right foot. Keep your back straight.

Now flex and point each leg in turn, without stopping in between each movement.

Contractions

The movement called a contraction is central to Graham technique. It gets its name from the contracting, or tightening, of the stomach muscles. This frees the pelvis and stretches the spine so they are ready for movement.

In its simplest form the contraction is a fairly small movement. You should be able to feel the movement even though it may not show very much. Try to imagine that you are lengthening your spine, not squashing it.

Clasp your hands in front.

Keep shoulders still . . .

. . . and directly over hips.

Sit cross-legged with arms out in front at shoulder height. To the count of three, tighten your buttock muscles, pull your stomach in, and push your pelvis forward.

Hold the contraction for a moment. Slowly return to the start. This is called releasing. Your body should not sag or slump as you do it. Repeat the exercise three times.

Centrework

Centrework exercises are done standing in one place. They aim to build strength in your limbs and back and to develop your sense of your centre of movement (see page 6).

You do centrework exercises both with your legs parallel and with your legs in a turned-out position, knees and toes facing out to the sides.

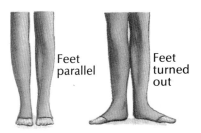

Feet parallel

Feet turned out

Parallel demi-pliés

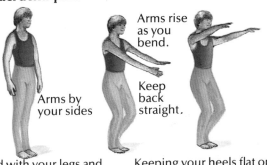

Arms by your sides

Arms rise as you bend.

Keep back straight.

Imagine you are pushing against the air.

Full plié

Arms straight up

Heels off floor

Stand with your legs and feet parallel, about 10 cm (4 in) apart.

Keeping your heels flat on the floor, bend your knees as far as you can.

Come back up, bending then pushing out your arms. Return to start.

Repeat three times. In class you will also do a full plié (shown above).

Leg beats

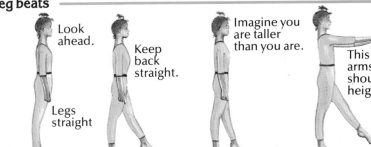

Look ahead.

Keep back straight.

Imagine you are taller than you are.

This time lift arms to shoulder height.

Foot comes back.

Legs straight

Stand with feet parallel. Slide your left foot out until it is pointed.

Then close it back to the starting position.

Now slide the foot out until it leaves the floor.

Bring the pointed foot back to the floor and slide it back to the start.

Moving in space

The exercise below is a walk to a three-beat rhythm, involving one long, low step and two short, high ones. As you do the exercise, imagine that your body topples forward but is caught just in time by the leg you are stepping on to. To help you balance, imagine the movement starts from deep inside.

Triplet

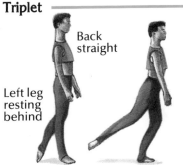

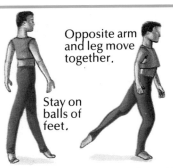

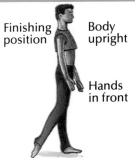

Back straight

Left leg resting behind

Legs straight

Opposite arm and leg move together.

Stay on balls of feet.

Finishing position

Body upright

Hands in front

Stand with your weight on your right leg. Take a long step forward on to your left leg. Bring your right arm forward.

Still moving forward, take a short step with your right leg, rising up on the balls of your feet. Move your left arm forward.

Then take a short step with your left leg.
Go straight into the next triplet taking a long step with your right leg.

Keep doing triplets until you are moving rhythmically. Finish neatly, with your weight on one leg.

Cunningham-based exercises

The exercises on these two pages are based on Merce Cunningham's approach to movement.

Cunningham does not write down his exercises in a final form. This means that he is the only person who teaches pure Cunningham technique, but these exercises will give you an idea of his dance method.

Cunningham's style emphasizes the upright position and these exercises are all done standing up. They aim to develop the suppleness of your spine and the strength of your legs. Try to move gracefully, with your arms and legs making neat, clear lines, so the movements look elegant.

Demi-pliés

All the exercises on these two pages involve doing a demi-plié, or knee-bend. This movement can be done with the feet turned out or parallel.

To do a demi-plié, bend your knees as far as you can, keeping your heels flat. Try to keep your knees directly above your middle toes. Keep your head up – this helps your balance. Imagine that you stay the same height, even though your knees are bent.

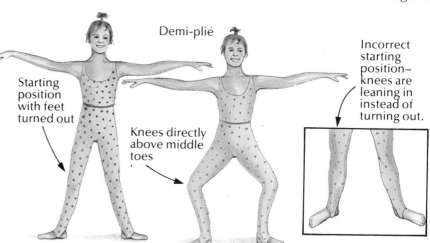

Demi-plié

Starting position with feet turned out

Knees directly above middle toes

Incorrect starting position – knees are leaning in instead of turning out.

Exercise 1

Hands turned inwards

Legs straight

Drop head and arms forward.

Arms at shoulder height

Demi-plié

Heels stay on floor.

Stand with your feet turned out and slightly apart. Hold your arms out to the sides at shoulder height.

Keeping your legs straight, curve your back out, so your upper body, or torso, drops forward to waist level.

Flatten your back until it is parallel with the floor. Open your arms out again and do a demi-plié (see above).

Keeping your back flat, straighten your legs. Bring your torso upright smoothly so you are back at the start.

Exercise 2

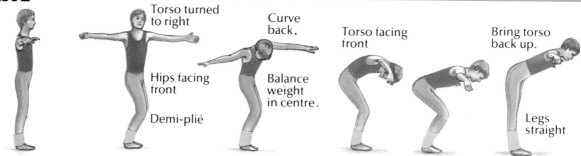

Torso turned to right

Curve back.

Torso facing front

Bring torso back up.

Hips facing front

Balance weight in centre.

Demi-plié

Legs straight

Stand with feet parallel and slightly apart. Hold your arms out to the sides at shoulder height. Look straight ahead.

Do a demi-plié and twist your torso to the right. Keep your hips facing the front and your heels on the floor.

Keeping your torso turned to the right, curve your back out. Then swivel your torso to face the front again.

Flatten your spine and straighten your legs out of the demi-plié. Then bring your torso upright again smoothly.

Exercise 3

Keep arms in same position.

Stand with your feet parallel, and your right arm held up. Bend forwards from the waist, curving your spine.

Hips face front.

Return to the start. Then curve your torso to the right. Keep your arms in the same position all the time.

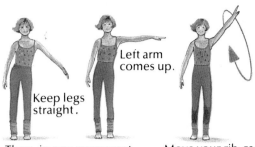

Keep legs straight.

Left arm comes up.

Then, in one movement, shift your rib-cage to the left, lowering your right arm. Bring your left arm out to the side.

Move your rib-cage back to the centre. Circle your left arm back and round, bending it as it comes up in front of you.

Arm bent

Demi-plié

Continue moving your arm up and do a demi-plié, tilting your head back so you are looking at the ceiling.

Arm finishes above your head.

Straighten your spine and legs. You are now in the starting position. Repeat the sequence on the left side.

Exercise 4

In this exercise you point your foot forward, to the side, to the back and to the side again. You make a semi-circle with your foot.

Then you do the same thing with the opposite foot, so that the whole exercise makes a complete circle (see right).

The first row of pictures below shows you how to do the sequence pointing your foot to the front.

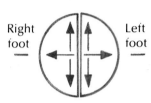

Right foot   Left foot

Work to a steady count, one beat for each movement.

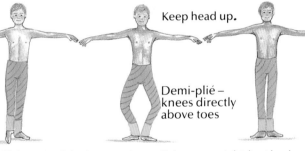

Look straight ahead.

Keep head up.

Demi-plié – knees directly above toes

Keep back straight.

Stand with your feet turned out, your heels together and your arms out to the sides.

Slide your right foot out in front and point it. Pull up on the muscles of your left leg to help your balance.

Bring your right foot back to the start and bend your knees in a demi-plié. Then straighten your knees.

Point the foot out again, and close back, but this time keep your legs straight as you close back.

Left arm as before

Remember to point twice.

Now repeat the sequence, but pointing your right foot out to the side, with your right arm curved out in front.

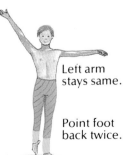

Left arm stays same.

Point foot back twice.

Repeat the sequence pointing your right foot out behind. Hold your right arm up in a diagonal line.

Finally repeat the sequence pointing the right foot out to the side again. Hold the right arm curved out in front.

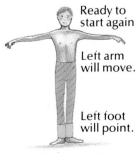

Ready to start again

Left arm will move.

Left foot will point.

Do the whole exercise as before, but pointing the left foot and moving the left arm instead of the right.

15

Jazz dance

Jazz dance is energetic and expressive. It is great fun to do and improves your co-ordination. Nowadays, most of the dance you see in musicals, films and pop videos is jazz dance.

You can be any shape or size to do jazz dance. It is best to start learning when you are about 13 and your bone structure has grown quite strong. This is because jazz movements put a lot of stress on the spine and pelvis. Make sure you go to a fully qualified teacher.

Jazz dance has some very distinct characteristics. You can find out about four of these below.

Rhythm

Rhythm and co-ordination are the most important aspects of jazz dance. You need to be able to express the rhythm of the music in your movements. When you start jazz classes you usually dance to pop music which has a strong, simple beat. True jazz music has more complicated rhythms.

Syncopation

Listen to a piece of music and clap in time to it. Now listen again but this time clap in between the beats. You are syncopating the rhythm. This is an important skill in jazz dance. As you practise syncopating you will learn to hear all the possible rhythms of the music you dance to.

Hip swinging

Jazz dance includes many hip and pelvic movements, which are used to reflect rhythms and make expressive poses. Swinging your hips also helps to develop the quick reaction to rhythms which is essential in jazz dance.

Isolation

An isolation is moving one part of the body while keeping the rest of it still or moving in a different direction. Like hip swinging, this emphasizes the rhythms of the music by repeating them with the body. It looks as if the music is played right through you.

Isolation has become a very sophisticated skill which is also used by body poppers (see page 30).

Different types of jazz

Jazz dance is always changing, partly because it allows dancers to make up their own steps and because it is danced to various kinds of music.

There are several distinct styles. One of the most popular is Rock or Funk Jazz which is danced to pop music. It is a powerful, dynamic style which is taught in many jazz classes today.

There are three, more specialized styles called Traditional, Gospel and Afro-Caribbean Primitive. These are quite similar to the earliest forms of jazz dance created by Africans (see opposite).

Broadway Jazz is a more polished, flamboyant style. It developed when jazz dance became a form of professional entertainment in the 1920s. It is named after Broadway, a street in New York where there are lots of theatres and dance shows. Broadway is a glamorous, punchy kind of jazz which is exciting to watch.

Learning jazz

Many jazz classes are available in studios, schools and dance colleges. Although jazz dance can be very free and creative, when you start you have to concentrate on learning the technique and basic steps.

Like other kinds of dancing, jazz is a discipline in which you need to control your body. You learn to move with and interpret the music.

The main thing is not to get impatient or discouraged. Be prepared to feel quite hopeless and silly in class for a few weeks. If you persevere you will have lots of fun. With practice you will be able to make up your own jazz dances and as your technique improves, you can try more specialized styles.

Jazz music

Jazz music developed with jazz dance as part of the new black culture in America from the 17th century onwards. The main jazz instruments are saxophone, piano, double bass, trumpet and drums. The music has varied rhythms and great energy which make you feel like dancing. For many years jazz dance was performed only to jazz music, but since the 1940s it has been danced to other types of popular music with good rhythms.

At the back of this book there is a list of records which have exciting rhythms to dance to. Listen to a few and see which ones make you want to get up and dance.

The African roots of jazz

Jazz dance developed from African tribal dances. These were brought to the Caribbean and to America by African slaves in the 17th and 18th centuries. Over the years the slaves' dances were influenced by dances from the cultures in which they were forced to live.

During the 19th century, entertainments known as minstrel shows developed, involving singing and dancing to jazz music. At first they were performed only by black dancers for black audiences.

Then in the 1920s jazz music and dancing became hugely popular with both blacks and whites and spread to Europe. The minstrel shows were taken over by professional dancers who brought new skills and training to the jazz style.

At the same time movements from European dances such as the Foxtrot were gradually blended into the jazz style.

As popular music changed in the 1940s and '50s so did the dancing and it was during this period that modern jazz styles evolved.

17

Jazz exercises

On these two pages there are some jazz exercises to try. Each teacher interprets jazz techniques in an individual way, so you may learn different exercises at your class.

It is best to do the exercises in the order in which they appear here, because this will help your body get used to the sort of movements involved.

The stretch exercises improve suppleness by stretching out your muscles.

Then the isolation exercise teaches you how to move one part of your body separately from the rest of it. You can then go on to do more dramatic moves, such as the jazz turn and walk.

Stretch Exercise 1

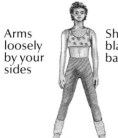
Arms loosely by your sides

Shoulder-blades back

Knees stay bent.

Hands touch floor.

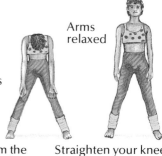
Arms relaxed

Stand with your feet wide apart and parallel. Then bend your knees and push your bottom out. Drop your head back.

Bend forward from the waist and hollow the lower part of your spine. Keep your shoulder-blades back but relaxed.

Lean right down from the waist, letting your back curve outwards. Drop your head and arms forward.

Straighten your knees and spine, gradually bringing your torso upright so that you are back in the starting position.

Stretch Exercise 2

Shoulders down and relaxed

Torso faces front.

Don't tilt head up.

Relax arms.

You can bend your knees slightly to help you.

Stand with your feet turned out, wide apart and your arms straight up. Stretch to the right.

Keeping your back straight, bend from the waist so that your torso is parallel with the floor.

Pull your leg muscles up, and reach down over your right leg so your hands touch the floor.

Swing your torso across to the centre, so your head and arms are dropped loosely between your feet.

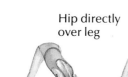

Hip directly over leg

Back flat

Legs straight

Swing your torso through to the left side, so you are reaching over your left leg. Make sure your back is flat.

Swing your torso up so it is parallel to the floor, pointing to the left. Straighten your arms.

Then bring your torso up to the left, so you are looking to the front while stretching to the left.

Bring your torso upright to return to the start. Repeat the sequence, this time stretching to the left first.

18

Pelvic isolation

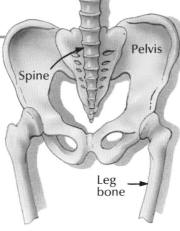

Spine

Pelvis

Leg bone

The pelvis is the circle of bone formed by your hips. It joins your leg bones to the base of your spine.

The pelvis is used a lot in jazz dance. It acts like a lever pushing your back or legs into action. It also links movements in your torso with movements in your legs, to make a flowing sequence which runs through your whole body.

To use your pelvis in these ways you need to be able to move it separately from the rest of your body. The exercise on the right and below shows you how to do this.

Starting position (front view)

Hands splayed out

Stand with your feet slightly apart and parallel, your knees bent and your elbows tucked in.

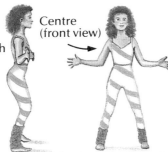

Starting position (side view)

Don't overarch your back.

Centre (front view)

Make moves small and precise.

Tilt your pelvis forward. Bring it back to the centre. Try to keep the rest of the body still.

Tilt your pelvis back slightly, so your bottom juts out. Return to the centre.

Push your pelvis to the right, so your right hip nearly touches your elbow. Return to centre.

Push your pelvis left and return to centre. Now repeat the whole sequence four times.

Jazz step turn

Hold arms as you like.

Bend forward slightly.

Head comes up.

Straighten back.

In this exercise you do a complete turn. Start with your feet together. Step out on to your left foot.

As you step on to your left leg, pivot on your left foot and then step on to your right leg.

Pivot on your right foot, bring your left foot round to the left. Finish with your weight on your left foot.

Bring your right foot to join your left, so you are back at the start. Now go back the other way.

Jazz walk

Lift right heel off floor.

Straighten left leg.

Move arms as you like.

Stand letting your weight sag to your right. Step to the left, pushing your weight to the right.

Bring your right leg to join your left. As your right foot moves across swing your weight to the left.

While your feet are together, shift your weight back to the right. Now step out again to the left.

Repeat the movements in a smooth sequence, so you travel sideways. Then go the other way.

Tap dance

Tap dancing is one of the most stylish kinds of dance and a fun way to exercise. It is a dance where you create your own sound with your feet so you do not need to rely on music. The main qualities you need are a good sense of rhythm and timing, and a love of performing to an audience.

The essential movements of tap come from your feet and ankles. Your arms, head and hands are important, but they move to complement the actions of your feet.

Tap styles

Tap is an American dance, but it has also developed in England with a slightly different style. The main feature of American tap, known as jazz tap, is the looseness of the body which makes the style look very fluid and elegant.

In England a European style of tap has developed which is more closely related to Irish and English clog dances. It is a bouncy style with the body held more rigidly.

Whatever the style, the important thing about tap is that dancers improvise and express themselves.

How tap started

Tap dance started in America in the 19th century. Its roots are in the Irish jig and English clog dances of early settlers, mingled with the African tribal dances brought by slaves. The European jigs involved intricate leg and footwork, while the Africans danced flat-footed, moving their whole body to the pounding rhythms of their drums.

Tap emerged when black slaves on the American plantations combined their rhythms with the jigs and clog dances. White people began to copy the black dancers and tap eventually became a performance dance. People started to wear special tap shoes with metal plates on the soles and to learn a basic technique.

Tap dancing reached the height of its popularity in the 1930s through Hollywood film musicals. These starred tap artists such as Fred Astaire, Bill Robinson, Eleanor Powell and Gene Kelly. Fred Astaire is probably the most famous. He was trained in ballet and his tap style is distinctively graceful and elegant.

Tap shoes

Toe tap

Heel tap

You can buy special shoes with toe and heel taps or have taps fitted to ordinary shoes. The shoes should be soft and flexible, should cover your whole foot and have a slight heel. (Stilettos or sling-backs are no good.)

Before you buy any shoes make sure they fit you very well and that you can bend your toes up when you are wearing them.

The best clothes to wear for tap are a leotard and tights or loose-fitting trousers and a top.

Music for tap

Tap dance was first performed to jazz music and is best suited to the irregular rhythms of jazz. Jazz music changed over the years and so tap was done to Charleston music in the 1920s, swing music in the '30s and be-bop in the '40s.

Today people tend to tap-dance to music from old films such as "Singin' in the Rain" and "Tea for two".

Preparing to tap

Your feet do most of the work in tap dance and it is important they are warmed up before you begin.

Here are some warm-up exercises to try. For the first two sit on a chair or hold on to a support.

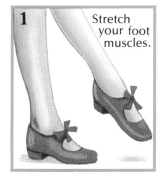

1 Stretch your foot muscles.

Start with your feet parallel on the floor. Lift your left foot off the ground and then point it down as far as you can.

Then bring your foot up as far as you can, flexing your toes. Repeat the down and up movement slowly, four times.

Do the same with your right foot. This exercise helps to strengthen your ankle, so you can tap with a clear, crisp sound.

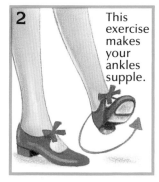

2 This exercise makes your ankles supple.

Raise your left leg and point your foot straight up. Circle your foot round slowly. Repeat the exercise four times.

Then circle your foot four times in the opposite direction. Repeat the whole exercise with your right foot.

3 Bounce eight times.

Stand on the balls of your feet and bounce up and down without leaving the ground or allowing your heels to touch the ground.

4

Try this exercise to practise using the ball of your foot separately from the heel. Walk to a steady rhythm lifting your legs a few inches off the floor in a strutting movement. With each step bring the ball of your foot down on to the floor first, then the heel.

As you take each step swing the arm opposite to the leg which is lifted.

Tap steps

To tap-dance you relax your body and strike the ground smartly with the ball or heel of your foot. The tap should make one clear ringing sound.

On these two pages there are some basic tap steps for you to try. Practise each one with both feet. When you have mastered the basic steps there are suggestions for putting several together to make a tap sequence.

Before you start

1. Make sure that you are practising on a good tap surface such as wood or hard linoleum. You can buy a special tap mat or make one out of a piece of plywood.

2. When you are tapping, count to a steady rhythm "1 and 2 and 3 and 4 and". Most of the time you tap on the number, but sometimes you tap on the "and" as well so you are tapping twice as quickly as usual.

3. Keep your knees and ankles as loose and flexible as you can and try to produce a clear, crisp sound when you tap.

Straight tap

Relax your knee.

Stand on your right foot. Extend your left leg so your foot is just off the ground.

Now strike the ground sharply with the ball of your left foot. Keep your knee still.

Finish the tap with your left foot pointing up and held off the ground. Keep your right foot still.

Forward tap

Keep hip and thigh still.

Use knee and ankle joints freely.

Stand on your left foot, with your right foot lifted up behind. Relax your knees.

Move your foot and leg forwards from the knee tapping the ground once as you go.

Finish with your right foot pointing upwards and held off the ground. Keep your left foot still.

Backward tap

Stand on your left foot and extend your right leg in front, pointing your right foot up.

Move your right foot backwards, tapping the ground once as your foot comes back.

Finish with your right foot just off the ground, toes pointing down towards the floor.

Shuffle

A shuffle combines the movement of a forward and backward tap as

shown in these pictures. It is done very quickly. Count a steady beat "1 and

2" and try to do the shuffle so you tap forward on "and", then backward on 2.

Hop

Stand on the ball of your left foot with your knee slightly bent and your right foot off the ground. Now hop, lifting your left foot clear of the floor and landing on the ball of your foot so that you make a single sound. Try not to wobble as you land.

Shuffle hop

This combination of a shuffle and a hop makes three tap sounds. Try it slowly at first. Tap forward with your right foot on 1, back on 2, hop on your left foot on 3 and hold the position for 4. Then speed it up: tap forward on 1, back on "and", hop on 2, hold for "and". Repeat on "3 and 4 and".

Arm positions

You can use lots of different arm positions when you are tapping. Here are three to try. Decide which looks and feels best by practising them in front of a mirror.

Parallel

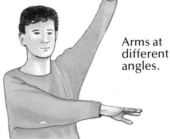

Arms point same way.

In this position both arms reach out in the same direction, without touching.

Co-ordinated

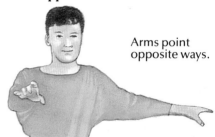

Arms at different angles.

Your arms are stretched out in the same direction, but at different angles to one another.

In opposition

Arms point opposite ways.

In this position your arms reach in opposite directions, one forward, the other back or out to the side.

Tap sequences

The following sequences are combinations of the steps shown on these two pages. As you do the steps, count steadily to eight as shown. The counts which are underlined are where the tap sounds occur. R stands for right foot and L for left. It is a good idea to do the sequences to music, so that you get used to dancing to a rhythm.

Sequence 1	
One	Forward tap R
and two	Backward tap R
and three	Forward tap R
and four	Backward tap R
and five	Shuffle R
and six	Shuffle R
and seven	Shuffle R
and eight	Step on to R
Repeat using your left foot.	

Sequence 2	
One	Forward tap L
and two	Backward tap L
and three	Hop R
and four	Step sideways on to L
and five	Forward tap R
and six	Backward tap R
and seven	Hop L
and eight	Step sideways on to R

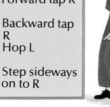

More tap steps

Here are the names of some more tap steps which you may learn at your classes.

Step A single tap sound made by stepping on to the ball of the foot.

Tap, step Two tap sounds made by doing a forward or backward tap followed immediately by a step.

Heel beat* A single tap sound made by raising the heel keeping the ball on the floor, then replacing the heel.

Tip of the toe beat A single tap sound made by raising the foot and touching the front edge of the toe tap to the floor.

Brush This is similar to a forward or backward tap but the movement is exaggerated by swinging the leg from the hip joint.

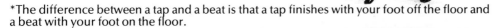

*The difference between a tap and a beat is that a tap finishes with your foot off the floor and a beat with your foot on the floor.

23

Rock 'n' roll

Rock 'n' roll first became well known in the 1950s when an American group, Bill Haley and the Comets, released a record called "Rock around the clock". American teenagers had  been dancing for some years to the heavy beat of Rhythm and Blues records that had been popular in the black community since the Second World War. New groups such as the Comets, and singers like Elvis Presley, took this music and mixed it with Country and Western to make the new sound – rock 'n' roll.

In America rock 'n' roll dancing is called the jitterbug and in Britain, jiving. Originally the jitterbug was a 1930s dance done to Big Band swing music. It was very fast and acrobatic. Now it is a slower dance, but still very exciting. You hold your partner's hand, spinning and turning.

The dance and music became a craze that spread world-wide from America.

Rock 'n' roll music

Rock 'n' roll music was fresh and lively. Most importantly, it had a simple, danceable beat and was aimed at young people. Between 1953 and 1959 lots of rock 'n' roll records were made, such as "See you later alligator" and "Don't step on my blue suede shoes".

A 1950s juke box

Rock 'n' roll culture

Rock 'n' roll shocked many people. It seemed wild and rebellious. A whole teenage culture grew up around it with people meeting in cafés and listening to juke boxes.

In the late 1950s rock 'n' roll became commercialized and stale and new dances emerged.

Dancing rock 'n' roll

In the last few years there has been a rock 'n' roll revival. Some clubs have special rock 'n' roll nights and you can learn the dance at classes. You only need learn a few moves to start with. Then you can gradually build on them by watching other people. Below and on the next pages there are some hints on dancing rock 'n' roll and a few moves to try.

Clothes

Girls often wear full skirts which swirl round, adding to the movement and energy of the dance. Flat shoes are important for safety when you are turning and jumping. In the 1950s girls tied scarves round their necks and wore short socks.

Boys also wear 1950s style dress - baggy shirts with narrow ties, narrow trousers or denim jeans and suede shoes. In Britain a special style of dress was developed by "teddy boys" who wore long jackets, skin-tight "drainpipe" trousers and pointed shoes called winklepickers.

How to hold your partner

Here are the main rock 'n' roll holds. Partners start close together, then break away so they are at arm's length with elbows slightly bent. This gives leverage for movement. The boy moves with his legs slightly bent and shoulders hunched forward in order to provide a stable pivot for his partner. The girl does freer movements.

Closed hold - like a conventional ballroom dancing hold.

Double hold - you hold both your partner's hands.

Open hold, opposition arm - the boy's left hand holds the girl's right or vice versa.

Open hold, same arm the boy's right hand holds the girl's right hand or vice versa.

How to move your feet

Rock 'n' roll music has four beats to the bar. Your feet move in slow or quick steps. A slow step takes two beats and a quick step one.

The basic sequence of steps is shown on the right. It takes six beats (1½ bars) to complete and you repeat it over and over. These instructions are for a girl. For a boy the steps are the same but you do them with the opposite legs.

Over the page you can see how it looks when both partners do the steps.

Step right.

Step left.

Step back.

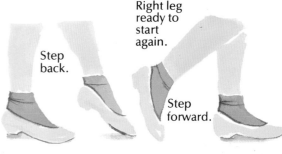

Right leg ready to start again.

Step forward.

Start with your feet slightly apart. Counting 1, 2, step sideways on to your right foot, so your weight is on your right leg.

On 3, 4, step sideways on to your left foot, shifting your weight on to your left leg. (These two are slow steps.)

Then, on 5, step back on to your right foot and on 6 step forward on to your left. (These two are quick steps.)

Dancing rock 'n' roll

On these two pages you can find out how to do some rock 'n' roll moves. They are all done to a count of six. The first row of pictures below shows the steps you do with your feet (see also page 25). The other rows show moves which you do while doing these steps.

You may find it difficult to combine the footwork and moves at first. If so, don't worry about what your feet are doing, just try to get the moves right.

The basic step

Step sideways on 1,2 (left for boy, right for girl).

Step sideways on 3,4 (right for boy, left for girl).

On 5 both step back, moving away from one another.

On 6 both step forward, moving close together again.

A simple turn

Arms stretched out.

Lean back slightly.

Start in a closed hold. On 1, 2, both step to the side (boy to the left, girl to the right). On 3, 4, the boy steps on to his right foot and raises his left arm. The girl circles beneath, pivoting on her right foot, then stepping on to her left foot.

On 5, both partners step back (boy on to his left leg and girl on to her right). Pull away from one another and lean back.

On 6, both partners step forward (boy on to his right, girl on to her left) so your linked arms bend.

Slide break

  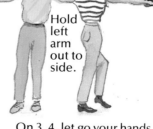 

Girl steps on to right foot, boy on to left.

Hold left arm out to side.

Start in a double hold. On 1, both raise your arms and turn to your left so you are facing in opposite directions.

On 2, still holding hands, bring your arms down so your left arm goes behind your head and your right arm behind your partner's.

On 3, 4, let go your hands and move apart, sliding your outstretched arm along your partner's outstretched arm.

On 5, pull away from one another, stepping back (boy on to left foot, girl on to right), then on 6 both step forward.

Spanish arms

Start in a double hold. On 1, 2, the boy steps on to his left leg and raises his left arm. At the same time the girl circles a half turn to her

left so she ends up with her back to her partner and her arms crossed in front. (Girl pivots on left foot, then steps on to right.)

Take small steps in order to get round the circle.

On 3, 4, the boy steps forward (right, left) and the girl steps back (left, right) so you move round in a circle.

On 5, 6, the boy steps back on to his right foot and raises his left arm. The girl circles right to get back to the start.

Push spin

Boy steps slightly to left of girl.

Hold right hands. On 1, 2, both step forward (boy on to his left foot, girl on to her right) and bend your arms.

On 3, the boy pushes against his partner's hand and she spins round to her right, pivoting on her right foot.

On 4, the girl completes her spin, stepping on to her left foot, and the boy catches hold of her right hand again.

On 5, 6, both partners step back (boy on to his left foot, girl on to her right) and then step forward again.

The Stroll

The Stroll is a group dance which is lots of fun to do. You stand in a line and everybody does the steps in unison. There are several different versions of the Stroll. In America the dance is done in two lines with girls facing boys.

Acrobatic rock 'n' roll

This is a mixture of rock 'n' roll and gymnastics with daring, athletic moves such as the Death Dive shown here. It was developed in Europe and is now a competition style. Couples from many countries compete in international championships.

Ceroc

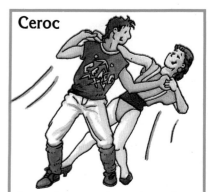

Ceroc is a new dance based on the French style of rock 'n' roll. The name comes from the French "c'est roc". Although many ceroc moves are similar to rock 'n' roll, the dance is more upright and precise with elements of jazz and tap.

Disco dancing

The term disco dancing covers a whole range of styles, from the dancing you do with friends at a party to complex, athletic routines performed at disco dancing competitions. What all the styles have in common is that they are done to fashionable pop records.

Most people learn to disco dance by watching and copying other people. However for competition disco dancing you need to train at classes in the same way as you would for other styles.

How disco dancing started

The first discos opened in the 1960s in France (disco is short for the French word "discothèque"). At these new clubs teenagers danced to pop records, rather than to live bands as they had always done in the past. Discos quickly spread to America and Britain, encouraged by the popularity of the new "solo" dancing (dancing without holding your partner). ▶

The Twist was the first solo dance. It was a simple dance in which you pivoted on one or both feet and swivelled your hips and knees from side to side, keeping your shoulders still.

A rock 'n' roller named Chubby Checker made a record called The Twist and the dance became a craze. The Twist was followed by other disco dances such as the Pony, the Frug and the Madison.

Disco dancing went through a lull during the hippie period of the late 1960s. It was revived again in the '70s with another dance craze and record called the Hustle, followed by the disco-dancing film "Saturday Night Fever".

In the '70s and '80s disco dancing has changed constantly with fashion and music. The main thing about it is that the movements are simple and repetitive so anyone can do them. There are no set rules and dances can be as simple or complicated and dramatic as the dancer wants to make them.

Disco clothes

To go to a disco you can wear almost anything that is comfortable and preferably a bit flashy. Most people wear bright, lively colours or smart white or black clothes.

For competitions, dancers wear leotards and tights, or, for boys, trousers that allow them to move freely but outline their movements clearly.

In competitions the dancers aim to outshine their rivals not just in their dancing but in their costumes, and the clothes reflect the glitter and glamour of a discothèque. Leotards and tights are made from shiny materials and are often highly decorated with coloured sequins or braid. They may have extravagant ruffles and wide, full sleeves which are tightly gathered at the cuffs.

Instead of tights, girls may wear sequinned stockings or legwarmers. They often wear glittery or beaded chokers and feathered head-dresses.

Disco dancing competitions

In 1977 following the revival of disco dancing an actor called John Travolta made the film "Saturday Night Fever" in which the hero and heroine win a disco dancing competition. The film made disco dancing hugely popular and the idea of disco dancing competitions spread to lots of different countries.

Competition disco dancing is quite different from most ordinary disco dancing. It is athletic and skilful with complex steps and routines. Dancers need to be fit and disciplined.

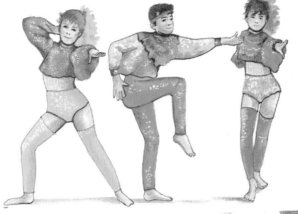

Competitions are organized into various age groups – under 12 years, under 16 years and adults. Dancers can compete as soloists, couples, trios (three dancers together) and teams.

The dancers compete for cups and different coloured rosettes which are awarded to the best performers. The cups may be quite elaborate, often featuring a picture of a disco dancer on a miniature shield.

Inside a disco

Today's discos are glamorous places with elaborate lighting and powerful sound systems. The disc jockeys, or DJs, who choose the music are very important because they set the style and the popularity of the club through their control over the kind of music which is played.

The disco sound

Disco music usually has a strong, simple beat which is easy to dance to. Special long versions of records are made called disco mixes. They last for about 20 minutes, allowing dancers to continue uninterrupted.

The sound quality of the records has to be very good because they are played over powerful sound systems. These have two or three turntables and a mixing deck. The mixing deck is a complex piece of equipment which allows the DJ to control the sound level, link or intermingle records and create special effects such as echoes.

Lighting

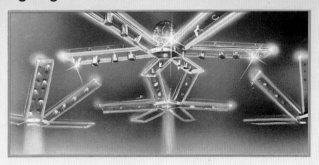

At first, disco lighting consisted of coloured light bulbs and balls with mirrors, hanging from the ceiling. As new clubs sprang up the competition for customers became fierce and lighting systems were one of the attractions.

Nowadays huge sums of money are spent on complex lighting systems, specially tailored to a disco's needs. These systems include laser beams and computerized control desks. Sometimes lighting is incorporated into or under the dance floor or into the walls to make unusual fantasy effects.

29

Breakdancing

Breakdancing began in the streets of New York in the 1970s and quickly became very popular. Many people learnt to do it by watching breakdancers and practising with them. You can take classes though at some dance studios. There are two different kinds of breakdancing, called body popping and breaking.

Warning: many breakdancing moves are very dangerous. Don't try them on your own.

Body popping involves moving like a robot but more gracefully. You move each of your joints in turn very quickly. Breaking is difficult and quite dangerous. Its basic moves are floor spins and glides. Below are a body popping move and a breaking move.

Body popping — the wave

Start with your right arm held slightly away from you. Jerk your right hand in so your elbow bends out.

Push your right hand inwards so your right shoulder is forced up until your head is resting on it. Keep your elbow bent.

Swing your head to the left and relax your right arm. Push your left shoulder up so your head rests on it and bend your left arm.

Push your left arm smoothly down and away from you. As your left shoulder comes down, push your chest out.

Flick left wrist up

Breaking — the backspin

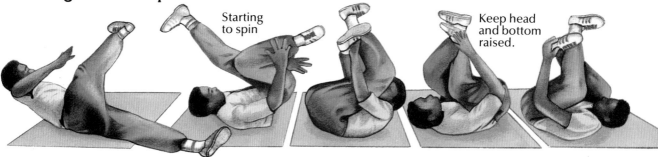

Starting to spin

Keep head and bottom raised.

Sit with your left leg stretched out, then lean on your left side. Swing your right leg up across your body, pushing your weight back.

Lift your head and bottom as your right leg swings up. Push off with your left leg and lift it off the ground. Bend your right leg in.

As you spin round, bend your left leg in. Cross your left ankle over your right so you form a tight ball. Clasp your feet with both your hands.

Tilt back slightly so you spin on your upper back, but keep your head up. Keep clasping your ankles to keep up your speed as you spin.

Breakdancing clothes

Most breakdancers wear loose-fitting, comfortable clothes that allow them to move freely. A tracksuit, or baggy trousers and a sweatshirt, are ideal. They wear tough shoes, such as trainers, tied with coloured laces to look smart.

For the more advanced moves, breakdancers need to wear knee and elbow pads, as well as a cap or hat to protect their heads when they do headspins.

Speaking the language

Breakdancing has its own special language which developed with the dancing, from words used by the street gangs in New York.

On the right there are some breakdancing words and their meanings. When you have read them, try translating what the boy is saying.

BAD .... good
BOX .... portable radio
BUCK .... brave
CHILLING OUT .... hanging around
COOL OUT .... relax
CREW .... dance group

DEF .... nice
DOGS .... sneakers, training shoes
FRESH .... marvellous, fantastic
HOME BOY .... close friend
JAM .... record, song
WACK .... terrible, bad
ZOOTED .... exhausted, pooped

I was chilling out with my def box.

Uprock

Uprock was one of the first types of breakdancing to develop. It is an aggressive battle dance used by some street gangs in New York.

In an uprock session, dancers from rival gangs compete against each other. The gang members form a big circle and the dancers stand in the centre. There they perform the most difficult and dangerous moves they can and the crowd decides who is the winner.

Many of the moves of uprock are borrowed from karate and other martial arts, but in uprock the dancers do not touch each other.

Breakdancing tips

Breakdancing is most fun if you do it with friends. For example, once you have learnt to do the wave (see opposite page), you can try passing the movement on to a friend who picks up the wave where you left off.

Another thing to remember is that breakdancing should be very expressive. Many breakdancing moves originally came from mime, which is a way of talking using your body. Try to make your breakdancing tell a story in movements.

Never try difficult or dangerous breaking moves without proper instruction from a teacher.

Music and dance

A famous choreographer*, Georges Balanchine, described music as "the floor the dancer walks on". Since the earliest times, dances have developed in response to music, changing as styles of music altered.

Music and dance are very closely connected through rhythm. A rhythm is a sequence of sounds and silences of different lengths. Dance is a combination of rhythm and movement, and music is a combination of rhythm and sound. We hear rhythms everywhere around us: in the chirping of the birds, the sound of the rain, or in a dripping tap. We also feel rhythms inside our bodies, in our pulse and in our breathing.

Because we are used to hearing and feeling rhythms, when we hear music with a strong beat, it is hard for us to resist the temptation to dance to it. In this way music and dance go naturally together.

Dance music

All sorts of sounds can create dance music. Today dances are performed to music played on anything from electronic synthesizers to dustbin lids.

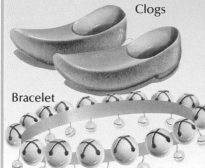

Electronic synthesizer

Clogs

In many dances the dancers themselves create the music by clapping, stamping and singing. They can make music by wearing costumes such as bracelets and clothes covered in bells, or special dance shoes, like clogs or tap shoes. They also use instruments such as tambourines.

Bracelet

Microphones

In some post-modern dances microphones are sewn into the dancers' costumes. These amplify the dancers' breathing and the rustling of their clothes, making a kind of weird music.

Rhythm and dance

All dances are based on some kind of rhythm. When music is written down, the rhythm is shown by the different kinds of notes on the stave. These indicate the length of each sound and of the silences between the sounds, showing the exact pattern of the rhythm.

Stave

Notes of different lengths

Although a choreographer may be inspired by the emotional power of a piece of music, the dancers' movements will mainly relate to its rhythmic patterns. These provide beats for the dancers to follow and so give shape to the dance.

Most choreographers like to commission new music specially for their dances, so they can choose the rhythms on which to base the dance. Sometimes, though, they use music which has already been composed.

32   *A choreographer is someone who creates dances.

How music helps dance

Dancers moving together rely on the beat of the music to keep in time with each other and to know when they should move. This is why, when you watch a dance, the dancers can move at the same time even though they may hardly look at each other.

Music also helps to create the mood of a dance. For example, rock 'n' roll music is lively, springy, and brash. It adds to the sense of fun and energy in the dance, which is full of quick, vivid spins, leaps, and swoops.

Dance without music

Some dances have no musical accompaniment. Instead, the choreographer gives the dancers a rhythm to follow, which they carry inside them by counting silently. This provides a kind of silent "music" which goes on inside the dancers.

Merce Cunningham, a contemporary choreographer, believes that music and dance do not have to be linked. He often creates dances done in silence, or only counting out a rhythm. In performance, there may be accompanying music, but the dancers still follow the rhythms they used in rehearsal.

Making your own music

You can make all sorts of different music yourself. You can use your body to make sounds, for example, stamping your feet or clapping your hands as you move.

You can also make simple instruments to give you a wider range of sounds to dance to. Below and right there are ideas for instruments to make using household objects.

Flower-pot drum

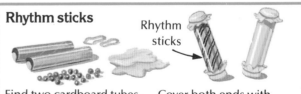

Drum

Stretch a piece of strong cloth or soft leather over the top of a flower-pot. Fasten the cloth tightly with elastic bands and sticky tape. Make sure it is taut. Use a wooden spoon as a drumstick.

Shaker

Shakers

Half-fill a plastic cup with dry rice. Tape another plastic cup upside-down over the top, so the two rims are pressed together. Shake to make a light rattling sound. If you like, decorate the shaker.

Rhythm sticks

Rhythm sticks

Find two cardboard tubes, like the ones inside rolls of paper towel. Fill them with pebbles or beads.

Cover both ends with pieces of cloth, fastened with sticky tape or elastic bands.

Peg xylophone

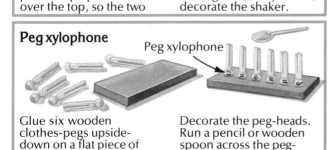

Peg xylophone

Glue six wooden clothes-pegs upside-down on a flat piece of wood or tough cardboard.

Decorate the peg-heads. Run a pencil or wooden spoon across the peg-ends.

See how many soft sounds you can make, and try to match them with gentle movements. Then try making loud noises and match them with powerful, lively movements.

Put the different kinds of sound and movement together to make varied patterns. Mix them with pauses and silences. You will be creating your own music and dance.

Choreography

Choreography is the art of creating dances. The term comes from two Greek words, "khoreia" meaning choral dancing to music, and "graphia" meaning writing.

Choreography is one of the most important aspects of dance. Every time you see a dance on the stage or TV, a choreographer has decided where and how each dancer should move. To do this, a choreographer uses many different skills.

Improvisation

Two dancers improvising

Improvising means acting on the spur of the moment, without instructions and with little time to prepare what you are going to do.

Choreographers often hold improvisation sessions to find out the various ways in which dancers could perform a particular movement. Improvisation often gives choreographers new ideas.

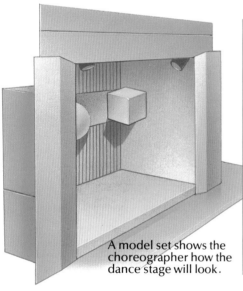

A model set shows the choreographer how the dance stage will look.

Dance notation

When a dance is choreographed, a special alphabet of signs is used to write down the movements involved in the dance.

These signs are called dance notation, or choreology. The two best-known kinds of notation are called Benesh and Labanotation.

Notation is very precise and enables a choreographer to preserve a work exactly as it was created. Learning to read and write notation is like learning a new language and takes a long time.

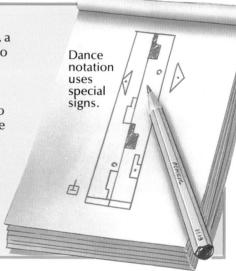

Dance notation uses special signs.

Learning to choreograph

To be a choreographer you need to know the various dance steps, why these were invented and what effects they can achieve on the stage.

Choreographers must also know how to use the stage space and must understand the basic principles of lighting and design.

Other important qualities are a good understanding of music, and plenty of imagination and original ideas. Choreographers also need to be able to work well with lots of different people and to be patient. It may take weeks to create a dance.

People often invent dances.

How choreography developed

Although people have been creating dances for thousands of years, choreography was only developed as a separate skill in the early 1900s.

As modern dance developed, traditions were overturned and the process involved in creating a dance was analyzed much more. People realized that choreography required special skills and it was recognized as an art form.

Nowadays it is possible to take courses in choreography and good choreographers are much in demand.

Creating a dance

Below you can find out about the main stages involved in creating a dance. Each choreographer has an individual way of working and the exact method used varies from dance to dance.

The first ideas

The choreographer decides on a subject for a dance. This may be inspired by anything, from a piece of music to a painting or book, or even a beautiful building.

The choreographer then chooses dancers to perform the work by holding auditions. Sometimes a dance is specially made for a particular dancer.

The choreographer and dancers explore the subject for the dance by having discussions and sometimes an improvisation session where they try out ideas.

Rehearsing the dance

The choreographer rehearses the dancers, all the time working out how the dance should develop and if it works as a whole.

As each sequence in the dance is decided, it is written down in dance notation by a professional notator, or choreologist.

The choreographer works with the lighting, set and costume designers, to produce the stage effects for the dance.

The performance

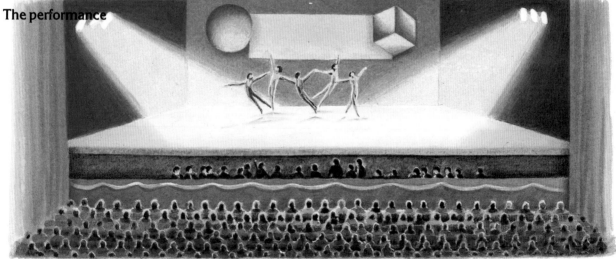

Eventually all the different elements are put together on the stage, and last-minute changes are made. The dance is now ready to be performed to an audience. This is the big moment: if anything goes wrong in the dance, the choreographer will probably get the blame!

Dance choreographers

On these two pages you can find out about some famous dance choreographers. They all began their careers as dancers, and then branched out to create brilliantly original dance styles. Even when their dances are expressing common ideas, great choreographers such as these find new ways of mixing movements together, so that dance itself never quite stands still.

Astaire's most famous dancing partner was Ginger Rogers. Their many films include "Top Hat" (1935) and "Swing Time" (1936).

"Swing Time"

Fred Astaire

Fred Astaire blended tap, ballet and ballroom dance techniques together to create a unique effect.

Astaire was born in Nebraska, America in 1900. He went to Hollywood in 1933 to appear in films. On film the subtlety and stylishness of his dancing came across very clearly. He was quickly recognized as an outstanding dancer and choreographer.

Although many of his dances were very complicated, he moved in a way that made them look effortlessly graceful.

Martha Graham

"Lamentation"

Martha Graham was born in 1894 in Pittsburgh, America. In 1916 she joined the Denishawn School of dancing but by 1923 had developed her own style.

She used strong gestures and positions that made the dancers look as if they were rooted to the earth.

Graham's dances were emotional dramas danced in a stark, ritual way. One example was her famous solo dance "Lamentation" (1930). Graham performed the whole dance sitting down, and wore a stretchy tube dress. This made her move in a way which looked restricted and painful, and which brilliantly suggested the deep misery which was the subject of the dance.

Other famous Graham dances are "Letter to the World" (1940) and "Appalachian Spring" (1944).

Alvin Ailey

Ailey is an American choreographer whose work is notable for its very intense emotional power. He uses big gestures like wide-open arm movements.

His solo for a woman dancer, "Cry", describes the history of black women in America.

"Cry"

"Revelations"

Another of his most famous dances is "Revelations", which is danced to Negro spiritual songs.

Ailey's company, the American Dance Theater, is skilled in many techniques including ballet, Graham, jazz and African dance.

"A Chorus Line"

Bob Fosse

Bob Fosse is a director, choreographer, actor and dancer. He was born in Chicago and began his career dancing in sleazy nightclubs.

Fosse has choreographed dances for many films and uses creative film techniques, for example, making it look as if the camera is dancing too.

His flamboyant dances are influenced by jazz technique. The most famous are in the films "Cabaret" and "All That Jazz" and the show "A Chorus Line"

Twyla Tharp

Twyla Tharp was born in Indiana, America in 1941 and has become one of the most original contemporary dance choreographers working today. Her dance style mixes movements which suggest tap, ballet and rock influences.

Tharp's dances often look very casual and relaxed. She uses movements which seem loose, such as big sideways kicks which make the dancer look as if he or she is about to fall over. But in fact the dances rely on very complicated systems of counts. They are intricate structures, which leave nothing to chance.

Robert North

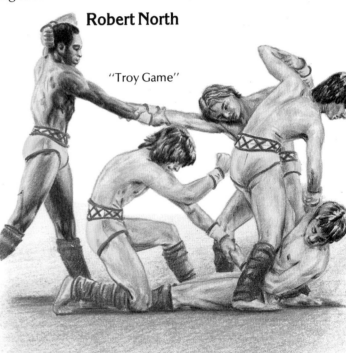

"Troy Game"

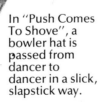

In "Push Comes To Shove", a bowler hat is passed from dancer to dancer in a slick, slapstick way.

One of Tharp's most famous works is "Raggedy Dances" (1972). It is full of attack and a sense of comedy which are typical of her work.

Robert North is an English dancer and choreographer who has worked with several major British contemporary dance companies.

His choreography is influenced by ballet technique and uses compelling music and themes which are easy to understand.

One of North's best-known works is "Troy Game", which is a funny, all-male display, involving fighting duets and athletic moves. It includes a role for a dancer who is smaller than the others and is always making mistakes. "Troy Game" is very lively and at the end the dancers fall down, apparently exhausted!

Dance companies

Most large dance companies* perform contemporary dance, for example, the London Contemporary Dance Theatre in England, the Wuppertaler Tanztheater in Germany, Paul Taylor Dance Company in America and the Australian Dance Theatre.

Groups performing other styles of dance, such as jazz and tap, tend to work in cabarets or places where they are hired for a season to perform along with comedians and other artists in a mixed show. Occasionally these groups perform in theatres.

Large and small companies

Company programmes and posters

Dance companies are much smaller than ballet companies. Even an important dance company has only about 50 staff, 15 or 20 of whom are dancers. Smaller companies have only about 15 members.

There are lots of even smaller dance groups which perform in places other than theatres. They bring dance to people who may not get the chance to see it in a theatre. They perform in schools, community or sports centres, prisons and old people's homes.

Touring

All dance companies tour, usually for about 30 weeks a year. Large companies go to each theatre for about a week. Small companies usually tour to different places every night.

Very few dance companies are based at a particular theatre.

One example is the Wuppertaler Tanztheater in Germany, which is based at the Wuppertal theatre. Other companies are based in dance centres which have rehearsal studios and staff offices but often nowhere to perform.

Jobs in a dance company

Opposite you can find out about the main jobs involved in running a dance company.

In large companies each job is done by a different person who may have several assistants. In smaller companies several jobs are done by one person and the dancers themselves take on many extra tasks.

Most dance companies are too small to pay for resident choreographers, designers and musicians. These artists are hired to work on specific pieces.

Artistic director

Musician

Wardrobe assistant

Lighting technician

Dancer

*This is excluding classical ballet companies.

Artistic director

All companies have an artistic director. This is the person who invites choreographers, designers and musicians to work with the company and chooses the dances, or "programme", to be performed. He or she also selects dancers to join the company and supervises their training.

In a small company the artistic director may also perform, take rehearsals and design costumes and lighting.

Company manager

This is the person who runs the company behind the scenes. He or she controls the company money. This includes paying dancers, negotiating contracts with choreographers and musicians and raising funds to support the company.

The company manager also finds places to rehearse, gets bookings at theatres, organizes tour arrangements and deals with last-minute crises, such as dancers injuring themselves or costumes getting lost.

Press and publicity officer

The press and publicity officer contacts theatres and discusses how to advertise the show, and gets posters and leaflets printed. He or she arranges interviews with the press and contacts local schools and dance centres to offer reduced price tickets.

The publicity officer also organizes the printing of programmes, t-shirts and badges which are often sold before the performance to promote the show.

The dancers

Dance companies are usually more democratic than ballet companies. There are no stars or principal ballerinas, so more dancers get the opportunity to perform solo or leading roles. In small companies five or six dancers perform every piece and there are no understudies or second casts. This puts the performers under more pressure but also gives them more work.

Dancers may also hold classes called workshops in local schools or dance centres to introduce the dances the company is performing.

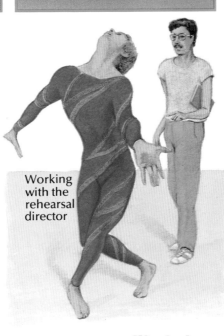

Working with the rehearsal director

Rehearsal director

The rehearsal director's job is to make sure the dances are performed well on stage. He or she watches rehearsals of new pieces, discussing the works with the choreographer and teaching new dancers their roles.

On tour the rehearsal director takes a rehearsal on stage in each different theatre, to work out how pieces will be performed on that particular stage. He or she also keeps the company up to scratch by taking notes at each performance and giving them to the dancers the next day so they can make corrections.

Checking the lights

Stage manager

This is the person responsible for getting the set built and the costumes made. He or she also makes sure the lighting and sound are ready for the performance, and that the scenery is properly in place. The stage manager also works out the rehearsal schedule.

On tour the stage manager discusses with each theatre manager the lighting and stage space needed for the dances.

Wardrobe manager

The wardrobe manager makes and maintains the dancers' costumes, washing and mending them. He or she needs to be able to sew skilfully and make costumes according to a designer's sketches.

In small companies dancers often make the costumes themselves.

Staging a dance

Staging a dance means getting it ready to perform to an audience. This involves much more than rehearsing the movements: normally, the dance needs lighting, costumes and a set. These add a lot to the performance.

Preparations

The lighting, set, and costume designers work closely with the choreographer while the dance is being prepared. However it is not until the dance is nearly due to be performed that all the different elements are brought together.

In the week before the first performance, there is a special technical rehearsal on the stage. The dancers "mark" out their movements so that the designers can check that the lighting, sound and set fit exactly with the dance.

Then there is a dress rehearsal where the dance is performed exactly as if to an audience, with the dancers wearing their costumes. This is an exciting moment: everyone sees the overall effect of the dance for the first time. It is also the last chance to change things that do not work.

The proscenium arch is the frame around the front of the stage.

Scenery

The **backdrop** is a large canvas cloth which hangs at the back of the stage. It is usually painted with a scene to create a background for the dance.

Tabs are curtains hung at the sides of the stage. They are sometimes drawn across the stage to separate it into different sections or to hide parts of it from the audience.

Wings are the spaces at the sides of the stage, in between the tabs. The dancers wait here to go on stage. When they stand in the wings they are hidden from the audience.

The stage

Dance stages vary from elaborate structures with proscenium arches (see picture) to bare spaces containing only the dance floor and stage lights. Some stages are raised above floor level. Others are on the floor, with the audience seating "raked". This means it rises in tiers above the stage level.

The best size for a dance stage is from 10m (33ft) deep by 10m across to 15m (49ft) deep by 15m across. It should have a smooth, even surface. The stage area can be altered by moving the tabs, or by positioning flats (see picture) in different places. Very big stages may have sections which can be made to revolve, or raised or lowered to create different levels.

The lights hang from a grid high above the stage.

Flats are large wooden frames with canvas stretched tightly over them and tacked down. Scenes are painted on the canvas to create different settings for the dance. Flats stand on metal struts and can be moved round the stage.

Strut

Costumes

Lighting

The lighting for a dance should make the shapes of the dancers' bodies stand out, to show each movement clearly.

Different coloured lights help to create the moods in the dance, and suggest the time of day and the season in which it is happening. Red and amber give a warm feeling, while blue makes a cool, wintery impression.

The whole mass of lighting equipment is called the rig. The grid is the network of metal bars from which the lights, called lanterns, are hung.

An enormous range of lighting effects can be created using different types of lanterns.

Flood light

Profile spots, for example, give out strong beams of light which can focus on particular areas. Fresnel spots give a gentler light which covers a wide area. Flood lights produce wide beams.

Fresnel spot

Profile spot

The set

The set of a dance is made up of a backdrop, flats and scenery, such as tables and chairs. Its purpose is to suggest the place in which the dance is happening. A set is specially designed for each dance.

The set designer makes detailed plans and often builds a scale model of the set which helps to show what it will look like and how

it should be constructed. The full-size set is then built by skilled craftsmen.

Because dance fills a stage very well on its own, dance sets often use little more than a backdrop, coloured lighting effects and a few flats. The set must always leave plenty of room for the dancers to move around freely.

Costumes

The most important thing about a dance costume is that it should let the dancer move freely. Dance costumes are often made of stretchy fabrics which outline the body shape and allow the dancer to move in any direction.

Costumes also affect the look of the dance movements. Light, flowing fabrics produce airy, graceful effects. Heavy fabrics cut in sharp shapes create a strong, more severe impression.

Special effects can be produced by decorating the costumes, for example with feathers or sequins. Brilliantly coloured costumes can give a dance a vivid impact.

Sport and dance

Sport and dance are similar in many ways. Both build up your physical strength and teach you self-discipline. They help you move in a precise way. In dance you move accurately to make your meaning clear. In sports like tennis and baseball, the more precisely you move to hit the ball, the better you are at the sport. If you already play sport this will help you when you learn dance, just as doing dance will improve your sports skills.

Useful dance skills in sport

Dance increases your suppleness, helping you stretch further and bend more easily. This is an advantage in a sport like tennis where you have to stretch out suddenly to reach the ball.

Learning to dance shows you how to fit your body into different spaces, for example, how to move neatly in a small space, and how to reach up into the air. These skills help you in games like basketball, where you need to jump high and dodge round your opponents.

Dancing in groups helps you in team sports, by making you more aware of other people and how to fit your movements to theirs.

Dance in ice-skating and gymnastics

Two sports where dance has had a big influence are ice-skating and gymnastics. In both these sports, the body is treated almost as an object.

In gym it has to be twisted, stretched or thrown through the air and caught up again, almost like a rubber ball.

In skating the body has to be manipulated to make interesting patterns.

This approach means that although good skaters and gymnasts may be able to move in a way that is technically impressive, they do not always put a lot of feeling into their movements. Dance can help them add warmth and flair to their routines.

Dance and the martial arts

Sports such as judo, karate and Tai' Chi are called martial arts. They began in the Far East long ago as a means of self-protection, using the body as a weapon.* Like dance, they aim to develop control of the body and the mind together.

For this reason Tai' Chi particularly is now often learnt by contemporary dancers. It is a very graceful and controlled technique, with unusual movements. Just as words from foreign languages can sometimes express our ideas or feelings more clearly than our native language, contemporary dancers find that Tai' Chi can add expression and variety to their dance style, or "movement vocabulary".

*The word martial comes from Mars, the Roman god of war.

Dance therapy

Dance therapy is a form of treatment in which dance is used to help people who have mental and physical handicaps. It is also used to help people who have had difficulties in learning, or in fitting in to society, and to relieve people who are emotionally disturbed.

How dance therapy works

The theory behind dance therapy is that the mind and body cannot be thought of as two completely separate things.

Your state of mind affects your body, and your physical health affects your state of mind. If you are unhappy, you won't feel like running around or leaping in the air. Your movements will probably become slow and very small. And if your body is ill or injured, you will probably feel quite depressed.

Dance therapy helps you to release tension, fear or frustration by moving your body.

It helps people with physical handicaps such as blindness or deafness to communicate with other people. Dance is a kind of language using the body. When we are very young, before we learn to talk, we use movements to speak to people. In the same way, when people dance together in harmony, they are talking to one another through their bodies.

How different people benefit

Through dance, blind people can become aware of the size and shape of their bodies and how they can move in the space around them, so they move with more confidence. By dancing with other people they can also get to know through touch what they are like.

People who are deaf have trouble learning to speak because they cannot hear the sounds to imitate. Dance helps them communicate through gestures.

Mentally handicapped people often have difficulty in concentrating for long. This may stop them from learning new things. Because dance is fun, doing dance movements encourages them to get into the habit of concentrating longer. By repeating particular movements they learn how to remember them.

Gradually they are able to learn more complicated sequences and this helps develop the memory.

Blind people can gain confidence by doing movements with others.

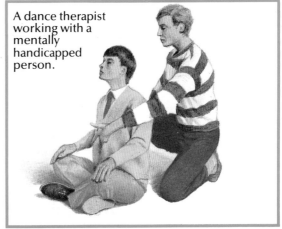

A dance therapist working with a mentally handicapped person.

Dance as a profession

To be a dancer you need a wide range of skills and a readiness to do all sorts of work, from performing in cabarets to appearing in TV commercials. There are very few opportunities to join dance companies and most dancers are freelance, taking whatever jobs come up and sometimes travelling abroad to find work.

Dance companies

Many dancers dream of joining a company. Large dance companies often have their own dance school. Each year they select just one or two of the dance students to join the company. The other dancers may find jobs in smaller companies, or form their own groups to get performing opportunities.

Musicals and shows

Some musicals, such as "A Chorus Line", are performed by dancers. Dancers are often needed for seasonal shows too, such as Christmas pantomimes or summer shows at holiday resorts.

For musicals and shows you need to be trained in all kinds of dance and you often have to sing and act, too.

Cabaret

Cabaret acts usually involve a lot of dancing. They are performed in discos or night clubs. The acts are fast and energetic, lasting for only about 15 minutes each night. The dancers may also perform feats such as fire-eating.

Cruise ships employ dancers to perform in cabarets to entertain passengers.

Musicals

Shows

Film

SLATE
USBORNE
DANCE.

Advertising

VIDO

TV

Video

TV and film

You often see dancers backing singers or other entertainers in TV shows. Some TV dramas and films require dancers as extras. Since the 1970s there have been some very popular films about dancers, including "Saturday Night Fever", "Flashdance", "Footloose", "Beat Street", "A Chorus Line" and "Fast Forward".

Pop videos

The pop videos made by bands to promote their records in discos and on TV provide another source of dance jobs. In these videos dancing is often combined with skilful camera work to create exciting images.

Because pop videos vary a lot, the dancers may get the chance to do several different styles of dance.

Business

Advertising companies use dancers in television commercials to promote products such as paint, drinks or sweets. Clothes designers also sometimes use dancers to launch their new collections at fashion shows.

These jobs can be very interesting, especially if you get work in a variety of adverts or shows.

Training

Most dancers start their training by taking ballet classes when they are young. Ballet technique is a good basis for any kind of dance. Some students even attend full-time ballet school before switching to dance.

If you want to join a dance company you must train for several years at a dance school, which you can join at about 16 or 17 years old. The competition for places is fierce.

For work in musicals and shows you need a wide range of performing skills, including acting and singing as well as dancing. You can get this kind of general theatre training at special theatre schools which take pupils from the age of about 11 or 12.

Finding work

A dancer with a company has regular work, but in other fields the work is intermittent. A job may last for one day, or a few weeks, or for months.

To get jobs, dancers attend auditions. These are rather like interviews where you perform in front of a panel of selectors who are looking for dancers to work in a particular show, video or TV commercial.

Many dancers pay an agent to get auditions for them. Dancers who do not have an agent have to find out about auditions for themselves, either from dance magazines and newspapers or by word of mouth.

Other careers in dance

Not everybody wants or is able to be a professional dancer. It is now possible to study dance as an academic subject as well as a performing art, learning about its history, its role in society, the art of choreography, dance notation, dance criticism and anatomy. This type of course gives you some of the skills you need to work in jobs connected with dance, such as those described below.

Administration

Dance administration is the work involved in running a dance company or dance centre or theatre. This includes organizing the finances and for this kind of work you may need a business qualification as well as a knowledge of dance.

Teaching

Dance is widely taught in schools, colleges and dance or sports centres. You can get specialist teaching qualifications, but these are not always necessary. A new job related to teaching is that of "dance animateur". This is someone who visits schools, community centres and old people's homes, introducing dance to all age groups and encouraging interest in it as a creative activity.

Dance therapy

Dance therapists work in hospitals and special schools. They use dance to help handicapped people (see page 43).

Dance therapy is a fairly new field but there are a few training courses available.

Dance notation

Dance notators write down dances as they are being created. Being a dance notator is a highly skilled job and you need to take a special course in notation. These courses are available at centres such as the Dance Notation Bureau in New York or the Benesh Institute in London.

Dance words

Afro-Caribbean dance. A kind of dance which developed over many centuries in the Caribbean islands, from a combination of traditional African and European folk dancing. Afro-Caribbean dance has influenced jazz dance.

Alignment. The way you hold your body when you are dancing to create a graceful line.

Amalgamation. A term used in dance to describe a sequence which combines different kinds of steps.

Animateur. A dance teacher who goes to schools and community centres to introduce dance to people of various age groups.

Balance. A dance term which describes both holding your body in a stable position, and also the inner feeling that your body is working as a controlled whole as you move.

Ballet. A stylized, formal type of performance dancing. Ballet aims to create graceful patterns and involves rigorous training.

Ballroom dance. A popular form of dance done in couples. It was widely danced from the 1930s to the 1950s and is still done socially and for competitions.

Benesh notation. A code of symbols used to write down dance movements. It was invented by Rudolf and Joan Benesh.

Body popping. A kind of breakdancing where you move different bits of your body separately.

Breaking. An energetic, quite dangerous form of breakdancing where you do moves such as headspins.

Broadway jazz. A jazz dance style which has influenced the dancing you see in TV and stage shows.

Centre of movement. The dance term for the mid-point of your body from which dance movements start.

Centrework. Usually the second stage of a class in *Graham technique*, involving exercises done standing up.

Choreographer. A person who creates dances.

Choreography. The art of creating dances.

Choreologist. A person who writes down dances using a form of *dance notation*.

Choreology. The art of writing down dance movements in *dance notation*.

Contraction. A dance movement which involves tightening the stomach muscles in order to help the pelvis and spine move more freely.

Cooling down. The process of doing gentle stretching exercises after dancing so that your muscles relax gradually. This helps to stop you becoming stiff the next day.

Co-ordination. The way you combine movements so your body moves as a balanced whole, even though different parts may be doing different things.

Cunningham technique. A style of contemporary dance developed by the American dancer, Merce Cunningham.

Dance notation. A code of written symbols used for recording dance steps on paper. The most commonly used systems of notation are *Labanotation* and *Benesh notation*.

Dance slippers. Soft slip-on shoes with rubber or leather soles and soft leather or canvas uppers, which allow the foot to flex and point freely.

Demi-plié. A dance movement which involves bending your knees while keeping your heels on the floor.

Elevation. The ability to jump high into the air in dance.

Extension. The action of stretching out part of your body as far as you can.

Flexed foot. A position of the foot in which the ankle is bent and toes pulled back towards the knee.

Floorwork. Usually the first part of a class in *Graham technique*. It is done sitting, lying or kneeling on the floor.

Foxtrot. A popular ballroom dance which developed during the 1930s in America and involved quick, running movements across the dance floor. Some features of the Foxtrot were incorporated into jazz dance.

Gospel jazz. A special kind of jazz dance which is done to traditional gospel music like that sung by the black slaves in America in the 17th and 18th centuries.

Graham technique. A style of contemporary dance developed by the American dancer, Martha Graham.

Improvisation. Dancing or acting without having set steps or a script and with little advance preparation. Improvisation is used to explore different ways of expressing ideas in movement.

Isolation. A movement used in several styles of dance, such as jazz and breakdancing. It involves moving one part of the body separately from the rest of it.

Jitterbug. One of the earliest forms of jiving which was popular in America in the 1930s and '40s.

Jiving. A type of energetic rock 'n' roll dancing.

Labanotation. A code of symbols invented by Rudolf von Laban for writing down dance moves.

Limón technique. A style of contemporary dance developed by the Mexican dancer, José Limón.

Lock. The action of straightening the knee fully when you are standing up, so that your leg provides a strong support for your weight.

Long. A term used in dance to mean keeping a part of the body such as your neck or back stretched out straight, but not stiff.

Marking. Going through the movements of a dance routine without dancing them fully, in order to familiarize yourself with the steps before performing. Dancers also mark steps in a technical rehearsal, to show the lighting and sound technicians which parts of the stage will be used in the dance.

Movement memory. A term used in dance therapy to describe the sequences of movements a person can remember how to do.

Movement vocabulary. The range of different movements a dancer can do.

Moving in space. The part of a contemporary dance class where you do movements that take you across the dance studio.

Opposition. Moving opposite sides of the body at the same time. In the *triplet* on page 13, for example, your left arm swings forward as you step on to your right leg. The term can also describe arm positions in which the arms point in opposite directions.

Parallel. A dance position in which you stand with your feet and legs facing in the same direction, either close together or apart.

Pattern. A term used in tap dancing to describe the overall shape of a dance sequence.

Plié. A dance movement in which you bend your knees fully until you are very near the ground, with your heels off the floor.

Post-modern dance. The various kinds of contemporary dance which have evolved since the 1960s.

Release. A dance term for straightening the spine out of a *contraction*. The release should not be a collapse of the muscles. In a release position your back is completely straight.

Relevé. A dance movement in which you rise up on to the balls of your feet.

Routine. In dance, a term meaning a sequence of movements or steps.

Stamina. Your ability to sustain physical activity over a long time.

Stop timing. A term used in tap dancing when a dancer stops moving and holds a position while the music goes on playing.

Synchronization. Doing different movements at the same time, for example, clapping your hands while moving your feet.

Syncopation. The marking out of beats in a rhythm so that you bring out unexpected parts of the rhythm, for example, clapping in between the strong beats of a rhythm.

Tacit timing. A term used in tap dancing to describe a moment when the music stops and the dancers go on dancing, so that only the sound of their tapping can be heard.

Tempo. The speed at which a dance is performed or music is played.

Tilt. A dance position where you hold your body at an angle to your supporting leg.

Time step. A set rhythm or pattern of steps tapped out by your feet in tap dancing. Time steps are usually repeated several times and so used in routines to lead into more spectacular movements.

Timing. The way the movements of a dance fit the accompanying rhythm or music.

Traditional jazz. A type of jazz dancing which developed in America from vaudeville and minstrel shows.

Transition steps. Movements done in between different positions in a dance sequence or exercise.

Travelling step. A step in which you move across the floor.

Triplet. A dance walk done to a 3/4 beat.

Turned out. Term used to describe a dance position in which you stand with your legs and feet facing outwards. Your feet may be either together or apart.

Uprock. A type of competitive breakdancing done by gangs in New York instead of fighting with weapons.

Warming up. Doing exercises which stretch and loosen the muscles to prepare your body for dancing.

Records for jazz dance

For rock jazz

Almost any records by the following:

Michael Jackson
Grace Jones
Donna Summer
"Wham"
"Five Star"
Madonna
Matt Bianco

Songs from the albums "Jump" by the Pointer Sisters and "Let's Dance" by David Bowie.

Songs from "Fame", "Flashdance", "West Side Story", "A Chorus Line" and "Cats".

For funk jazz

Most records by:

Quincy Jones
Earth, Wind and Fire
George Benson

For soul jazz

Any records by:

Womack and Womack
Aretha Franklin
Sade
Stevie Wonder
Smokey Robinson

For traditional jazz

"Take Five" by Dave Brubeck
"Sing Sing Sing" by Benny Goodman

Any records by Duke Ellington (although these are probably too difficult for beginners).

Index

Usborne Publishing would like to thank the following for use of photographs and other material for artistic reference. Every effort has been made to trace other photographers whose pictures have been used for reference.

Page 2, centre left © Dominic Photography.
Page 4, top © Pineapple Group plc.
Page 8, top © Pineapple Group plc.
Page 11, bottom centre © Anthony Crickmay.
Page 36, top right © BBC Hulton Picture Library.
Page 37, top © Dominic Photography;
centre right © Anthony Crickmay.

First published in 1987 by Usborne Publishing Ltd, 20 Garrick Street, London WC2E 9BJ, England.

Copyright © 1987 Usborne Publishing Ltd. The name Usborne and the device 🐝 are trademarks of Usborne Publishing Ltd.